Paul's Ten-Point Design for
CHURCH HEALTH & GROWTH

Paul's Ten Point Design for

Church Health & Growth

Peter Masters

THE WAKEMAN TRUST
LONDON

PAUL'S TEN-POINT DESIGN FOR
CHURCH HEALTH & GROWTH
© Peter Masters
First edition 2002, under the title, *Do We Have a Policy? Paul's Ten-Point Policy for Church Health & Growth*
This edition 2019

THE WAKEMAN TRUST
(Wakeman Trust is a UK Registered Charity)

Wakeman Trust UK Registered Office
38 Walcot Square
London SE11 4TZ

Wakeman Trust USA Office
300 Artino Drive
Oberlin, OH 44074-1263

Website: www.wakemantrust.org

ISBN 978 1 908919 99 1

Cover design by Andrew Owen

Printed by Stephens & George, Merthyr Tydfil, UK

CONTENTS

Paul's Ten Point Design for

Church
Health&
Growth

'Prothesis'
— Paul's
Blueprint

'Prothesis' – Paul's Blueprint

But thou hast fully known my doctrine, manner of life, purpose, faith, longsuffering, charity, patience . . . But continue thou in the things which thou hast learned and hast been assured of, knowing of whom thou hast learned them (2 Timothy 3.10 & 14).

WHAT ARE OUR AIMS for the shaping of our fellowship and for church growth? In every walk of life, whether in the worlds of business, politics, education, or any other sphere, it is accepted that leadership must have a policy or a definite set of objectives. Remarkably, in the work of the Gospel, this is sometimes set aside as an inappropriate or unscriptural idea. Perhaps it is a reaction, and in some ways a good one, from the mechanistic and worldly methods of the church growth movement. However, pastors and churches cannot be 'drifters' on the ocean of circumstances, taking an unnavigated voyage through uncharted waters. We should not just preach the Word and hope that everything else will fall into place. The fact is that we are *supposed* to have a policy for the growth and maturity of our churches, and such a policy is spelled out in many ways by the apostle Paul. If we are pastors and church officers, do we have a clear outline of what we are aiming for in the leading and shaping of our church fellowship? Do we have an agenda or plan or framework of desired objectives? Are we pressing forward in its implementation?

If a church member were to ask, 'Pastor, what is your programme?' – would we be able to list our aspirations for growth and maturity? And would we be able to demonstrate why these were the right and scriptural priorities for our church? Or would we be among those who could only mumble broad statements, however noble, such as, 'Oh, our purpose is the promotion of evangelism, holiness and spirituality'?

Paul had a very definite policy, and Timothy knew exactly what it was. This is clear from Paul's words to him in *2 Timothy 3.10* – 'But thou hast fully known my doctrine, manner of life, purpose.' The word translated *purpose* is 'prothesis', which means a plan, design, purpose or aspiration, clearly set forth, exhibited or displayed. It refers here to Paul's plan and strategy for the conduct of his life and ministry, which was 'fully known' to Timothy, his pupil. Paul did not keep his strategy for the churches locked away in his mind, as if it were a secret or purely personal method. Having received it from God, this wise master builder displayed it before his junior workers, just as a craftsman would teach his apprentices, or a general would share a battle plan with his immediate subordinates.

Unlike some others, Timothy was approved because he carefully observed the methods of the apostle, realising that these constituted the inspired pattern for the churches for all time. Timothy took Paul as his model, and as far as we can see, there should never be any other model for ministers and churches. The apostolic example is our authority, and may be relied upon to give success in the work of building up churches. 'Continue thou,' commands Paul, 'in the things which thou hast learned.'

Timothy was put in possession of a ready-made, prescribed policy. He was not given scope to be creative, ingenious or individualistic in this matter, and nor are we. At the beginning of the writer's present pastorate nearly fifty years ago, a well-intending deacon made the remark that no obstruction should be placed in the way of the new pastor should his methods vary from those of his predecessor. It was to be expected, so this deacon felt, that a new man would have a completely different approach. He took the view that no two pastors were the same, and so the church must expect a different kind of ministry.

This was certainly a most helpful and supportive attitude, but was it well founded? Should ministers greatly differ? Would we expect great variation in the practice of medicine or surgery? Would we be happy at the idea that every practitioner developed his or her own highly individualistic procedures and techniques? Or do we prefer to trust the existing consensus approach, whereby the best knowledge and experience combine to produce a fairly uniform set of therapies? In the case of the ministry there is a once-for-all policy which should be the approach of every 'workman that needeth not to be ashamed'. Ideally, if one set of officers passes from the scene and another is raised up, the overall policy should not be interrupted any more than if one doctor replaces another in the local surgery.

Vagueness will not build thriving churches or sustain them. Nor will emphasis on only one or two of the great pillars of church life, such as sound doctrine or passionate preaching, because the right policy is a combination of scriptural aims, and all must be pursued. Paul had a clear, consistent, and copyable set of aspirations and objectives, and these stand today as a pattern for all who are exhorted – 'be ye followers of me' *(1 Corinthians 4.16; 11.1 and Philippians 3.17)*.

The following ten ideals are all sourced to the Lord Jesus Christ or to the apostle Paul. May these great objectives be an inspiration and blessing to readers, and, by the goodness of God, to many churches.

Paul's Ten Point Design for

Church
Health &
Growth

1

A
Worshipping
Church

POLICY 1

A Worshipping Church

EVERY CONGREGATION should be a true worshipping church, and this must be the highest aim of all church planters, pastors and leaders. The language of worship pervades all the epistles of Paul, and in *1 Corinthians 14* the apostle provides the clearest picture of God's people at worship to be found in the New Testament, together with vital practical instructions. We must build worshipping churches.

But what is worship? Never have there been so many 'forms' of worship within Bible-believing churches as there are today. First, there is *pleasurable worship*, which puts the believer's enjoyment in the chief place, whereas it is God's pleasure that comes first. Secondly, there is *worldly-idiom worship*, which borrows and adapts the current musical tastes of the secular world, with its rhythms, instruments, actions, and showbiz presentation, whereas the Lord says that whosoever will be a friend of the world is the enemy of God.

Thirdly, there is *informal worship*, in which casual, relaxed, often jokey, trivia-injecting worship leaders turn churches into sitting rooms, whereas God demands dignity, order, reverence, grandeur and glory in his Temple.

Fourthly, there is *aesthetic worship*, which imagines that music, instrumentation, dancing, vocal rendition (and even craftsmanship) are all valid expressions of worship in themselves, so that God is worshipped *by* and *through* these things, whereas the Saviour said that 'God is a Spirit: and they that worship him must worship him in spirit and in truth.'

Fifthly, there is *ecstatic worship*, in which people work themselves into highly emotional and semi-hypnotic states, as though worship consisted of achieving an out-of-this-world, mystical connection with God, whereas Scripture says we must pray and sing with the understanding *(1 Corinthians 14.15)*.

Sixthly, there is *shallow worship*, which reduces the hymns to choruses containing just a few elementary ideas, whereas the *Psalms* – the model for hymns of worship – deal with solid themes to the glory of God.

These distortions and perversions of worship have swept in over the last fifty to sixty years. They ruin churches and dishonour the Lord, and we should want to train our people to love worship which is grand and glorious in character. True worship is *words*, a fact that was bedrock knowledge to all Protestants until a few years ago! The Saviour's term 'in truth' means that correct worship must consist of intelligent sentiments flowing from a rational and sincere mind. 'In spirit' means that worship should have no physical rites, ceremonies or bodily actions.

Much of what has today become so common in worship fails this great definition and standard laid down by the Lord. It is not true worship, but a mixture of entertainment and emotional self-indulgence. Worship is words, whether said, sung or thought. It is intelligent. It is certainly not the experiencing of strange ecstasies with the rational mind switched off.

Ministers who lead true worship must be careful to ensure that all the biblical aspects of worship are included in services – in prayer, song and preaching. These are awe, reverence, adoration, thanksgiving, rejoicing, repentance, affirmation of Truth, learning, intercession, and obedient dedication. Ministers must say, 'He must increase, but I must decrease,' putting away vain self-projection, exhibitionism, superfluous interjections, and levity. They must have a worthy sense of occasion, and behave as though the King of kings is present.

The ideal service must be a time of privilege, awe, and wonder. Joy will most certainly be a major feature, but joy not put in a context of awe and not accompanied by times of serious repentance, with earnest submission and supplication, becomes inappropriate joy. If the one who leads in worship is a chatty, flippant, wisecracking person, any sense of the awesome presence of God will be inhibited and even forfeited. Worshippers, too, must avoid chatter, and trivialised domestic notices should find no place in the service, only a sincere greeting and simple announcement of main meetings for adults and children. Lightweight informality has its place in human relationships, but not in the worship of the ever-glorious, almighty Lord.

If we can build thoughtful, worshipping churches, the people will deepen in outlook, increase in *spiritual* enjoyment, and be greatly strengthened in humility. It is a fact that *informality* in worship produces unhumbled, unawed, proud Christians. So does *aesthetic worship* (in which any offering of, for example, instrumentalism is like Cain's offering – something the worshipper has done, and can be proud of). *Ecstatic worship* produces pride in imagined spiritual accomplishment, and *pleasurable worship* induces selfishness and self-importance, as the worshipper (the 'customer') gets what he wants to enjoy.

True worship is what God enjoys; what he commands; what he is entitled to. At the same time it produces humble, unselfish Christians who are wholly submitted to God in deep appreciation and trust.

In other words, true worship sanctifies, whereas false, phoney and shallow worship is hostile to all that we long to see in Christian lives and in churches.

May the aim of every pastor and leader be to build a truly *worshipping church*.

Paul's Ten Point Design for

Church
Health &
Growth

2

A
Praying
Church

POLICY 2

A Praying Church

ANOTHER GREAT OBJECTIVE is that of building a praying church, the foundation stone of which will unquestionably be a worthy prayer meeting. Paul tells us repeatedly that he prayed without ceasing for all the churches where he had laboured,[1] and pleaded with them to pray for him. But how practical is our prayer meeting?

A distinctive gathering for prayer has a special warrant in the New Testament, where we see distinctive prayer meetings described in *Acts* chapters 1, 4 and 12. These were not preaching meetings, but prayer meetings, convened to besiege the gates of Heaven with specific needs. A special promise was set upon the prayer meeting by the Lord in *Matthew 18* – 'If two of you shall agree on earth as touching any thing that they shall ask, it shall be done for them of my Father which is in heaven. For where two or three are gathered together in my name, there am I in the midst of them.'

This promise (in a statement quite distinct from the Lord's

---

1   Eg: *Ephesians 1.15-16; Philippians 1.4; Colossians 1.9.*

preceding words on discipline) undergirds and mightily encourages prayer meetings. Spurgeon noted that in this text (and the promise of *Matthew 21.22*) the word 'things' is significant. These meetings will obviously praise God, and reflect on his majesty and goodness, but their primary purpose will be to pray for the specific ministries and concerns of the church. As Spurgeon insisted – they should be 'asking meetings', for this is what we are commanded to do throughout the New Testament.

In *Matthew 18* the Lord says God will especially bless if a number of believers 'agree' in prayer – the Greek word meaning 'sound together'. One speaks out audibly and the others follow in silent prayer. Then another contributes, and so on. To 'agree' also implies an agenda of concerns in which all have a common interest, and so the prayer meeting is not a gathering for stunning originality. It is chiefly a time when the ministries in which all are engaged, and the people they have on their hearts, are pleaded for.

Here are some practical standards for prayer meetings:–

- It is ideal to have a dedicated prayer meeting on a separate evening from the Bible Study.
- It is important that as many believers as possible attend, and that those who are able to pray aloud come with a high level of responsibility to do so.
- A list of special and regular concerns and ministries should be mentioned or read out before the prayer session begins.
- Participants should restrict their attention to not more than three concerns, so that many can contribute. If the main prayer session is 40 to 45 minutes, it follows that individual participants have only a limited time to pray. In a large prayer meeting of 100 people, 14-15 participants will be able to pray audibly as long as no one prays for more than three minutes. If someone were to pray for ten minutes, that person will have utilised a quarter of the meeting, which is clearly unfair (perhaps even proud). If the prayer meeting is much smaller, then longer

prayers may be appropriate. The meeting will be greatly enriched if the prayers are kept short enough for many people to be encouraged to pray. It is a wholesome practice to allocate the last ten minutes to very brief, 'one-matter' contributions.

- On the whole, pastoral-type prayers (petitions for holiness and conduct) should be the province of the officers or senior members.
- Participants should stand up to be audible.
- Any tendency to 'preach', exhort, complain or vent initiatives should result in kindly counselling by the pastor or an elder after the meeting.
- All the people should say 'Amen' in recognition of 'sounding together'.
- Participants should be encouraged to utilise all the time and not allow gaps to develop between prayers.
- If necessary, people should be privately encouraged to participate by officers.

If a fervent, committed prayer meeting can be brought into existence within a church, with many sharing responsibility in prayer, then the blessing of God will surely rest upon the efforts of that church, for the Lord has said, 'I will yet for this be inquired of by the house of Israel, to do it for them' *(Ezekiel 36.37).*

A good and practical prayer meeting cannot be achieved overnight. It may take time to wean some friends off their general prayers, or off their worldwide missionary tours, or off their cliché prayers, and so on. It may take time to train people into prayers which mention specific departments of the work, which lift up before the Lord individuals who are in need, and which focus on special endeavours such as visitation, personal witness, the Sunday services and Sunday School classes.

There are very great advantages in holding separate meetings for prayer and Bible study. A distinctive prayer meeting can be a much more intimate and powerful meeting. A fellowship may have some earnest but awkward friends who take time to adapt, and who dull the fervent 'edge' of the prayer meeting for some while, but this is what pastoral work is about – sitting down with fellow-believers, to explain the reasons behind an objective, and to encourage them along the right pathway.

Is the improvement of the prayer meeting part of our policy? It is most unwise to go knee-deep into evangelistic labours, rushing into one scheme and then another, if the prayer foundation is weak. We need much prayer for the preaching ministry. Every department of the work needs to be pleaded for every week. Are people and circumstances individually brought before the Lord? Is there an atmosphere of urgency, and are the petitions pressing and, above all, *specific*? This is how we prove the Lord. May he help every pastor and leader to build a truly *praying church*.

(More information on an ideal prayer meeting is given in the author's booklet, *The Power of Prayer Meetings*.)

Paul's Ten Point Design for

Church
Health &
Growth

3

A
Sanctified
Church

POLICY 3

A Sanctified Church

A NOTHER FOUNDATIONAL OBJECTIVE – vital if we are to secure the blessing of God in evangelism and growth – is that of building a *sanctified church*. This heading could equally read – a *well-pastored church*. There have been highly-acclaimed preachers who have not sought to *pastor* their churches, and their work has eventually fallen into disorder and confusion. How effectively do we pastor our churches to produce a sanctified community? Paul sets the standard in these words: 'Warning every man, and teaching every man in all wisdom; that we may present every man perfect in Christ Jesus' *(Colossians 1.28).*

There is so much to be done. Scriptural holiness must be preached; self-examination must be urged, and mutual admonition (in the right spirit) encouraged. We must strive to ensure that the church membership is as wholesome as it can be. When we receive in new members we must be extremely careful to ensure that they really love Christ and want to advance. And we must not turn a blind eye to the wrong behaviour of long-standing members.

The necessity of exercising discipline over a very serious offence should arise rarely in a well looked-after fellowship, but *all the time* we need to be watching out for the 'lesser' sinful attitudes which can hurt the offender and damage the purity and blessedness of the fellowship. This is not over-shepherding because it involves no high-handed intervention in the individual's private affairs. It is biblical watchfulness, undertaken by pastors qualified in terms of genuine respect and affection for their people.

Take, for example, the problem of gossip. Sometimes whisperings, carping criticisms and backbitings creep into a church. Do we have a pastoral concern about this? Not that we are to emulate the oppressive sort of pastor who leaps into action every time someone sneezes. That is so-called 'heavy shepherding'. We are not to engage in a pastoral overkill, interfering with every little problem as though Christian people had no spiritual power or conscience to regret their sin and put things right by themselves. Nevertheless, when people begin to gossip and run one another down, or to speak against the cause, then there is a sad and potentially serious problem, and someone will need to speak directly to those who have veered into this activity. They are probably helpable, but without help they could become a damaging root of bitterness. The question is – are the grumblers and gossips merely regarded as a nuisance, or is something done to help them? If the problem is caught early, then it may well be possible to resolve it in a spirit of friendship and respect.

Covetousness is also a problem which should ring alarm bells. What do we do if someone is plainly out of control and swept along by the power of desire? What if someone is justifying luxuries which will be a snare both to themselves and others? Do we talk to that person, help that person, and encourage him or her in the right path?

What if we pick up the signs that a great deal of TV watching has gradually crept into the lives of some members – including soap operas and other crass, worldly-entertainment programmes? Pastors and elders must be alive to things that they hear. People need instruction, help, advice, even warning, to keep them in the pathway of blessing. We are helpers in their joy, but are we functioning to this end?

It may be that suddenly there is a rash of parties among the young, and rather excessive socialising, involving showing off, banalities, and things of that kind. In a way, it may seem relatively innocent, but where is it going, and is it fitting in terms of the stewardship of time? Are those involved aware that even good leisure activities, while precious and profitable, should be subject to moderation, like food? Does anyone help those involved to appreciate such principles? Is there a pastoral or eldership touch on the tiller, or are faults allowed to grow into major traits?

Are there members who go visiting worldly places of entertainment, or engaging in fleshly, lascivious, modern dancing? These things could spread to others in no time, for the restraints of conscience are often broken by a bad example, especially if this is set by those senior to them in the Christian life. There are pastors who do not want to be involved with these things and who wash their hands of them. Their churches get into a serious state and then they flee to greener pastures, leaving others to clear up the mess.

What is our pastoral attitude concerning worldly dress, or worldly talk? We often encounter the problem of poor attendance. People mean well, but their attendance begins to be ragged and they gradually become less and less disciplined. Someone needs to get alongside and encourage them to come up to the mark before they slide too far for easy recovery.

Of course, many relevant exhortations will feature frequently in our preaching, but effective personal help still needs to be given by the company of office bearers. Tiny weeknight meetings are often the result of many years of neglect. No personal work has been done to keep members up to their spiritual privileges and duties.

Neighbouring churches sometimes pose a problem. Perhaps there is a nearby church with which our members should not be closely associated because of grossly unbiblical practices. Suddenly, some bright spark among the young people will think it wonderfully broadening and exciting to begin taking a little group off to meetings there. Novelty is always attractive. It is not an elder's job to become irritated and angry, but to explain to these friends why their activities are inappropriate. Furthermore, this needs to be done soon.

Hopefully the pastor will have fellow office bearers of gracious disposition who can help him in these responsibilities. Some can be officious and over-severe, taking the magisterial element of their office far too literally.

We should never insult believers by suspecting great sin or unspirituality the moment they slip into something wrong. We are to look for spirituality as the apostle did in *Philippians 4* when he counselled sensitive correction, saying – 'Help those women which laboured with me in the gospel.' Paul's first assumption was that they would respond to counsel, advice and help. Our immediate assumption must be that our members will be ready to listen. We must proceed with sincere respect, remembering that the discipline of the Lord is first kindly and only later progressive. ('My son, despise not thou the chastening of the Lord, nor faint when thou art rebuked of him.') It is paramount that we deal with things promptly. So many problems become serious and insurmountable simply because people were not guided while they were still dear friends in the Lord, and while they would still respect the help of others.

It is true that there are some preachers who take counselling to an extreme, and too much of their work is done by personal counselling. Many of the problems which have been referred to in these pages would be reduced to very manageable proportions if the preaching contained *practical* application to life, and conduct was addressed.

On a quite different note, we may have to deal with the case of someone who is engaging in blatant *subversion* in our church. Such a person is out to overthrow the order or principles on which the church is based. This is surprisingly common at the present time, judging from the reports of pastors. The intruding error is often charismatic, but not exclusively. The culprit may outwardly appear to be a very pleasant person, but he has an axe to grind or drum to bang. Maybe he has a contrary doctrinal viewpoint and he aims to oppose the teaching of the church. Or he may be a proud person who feels thwarted at not being made a centre of attention, or given office.

The subversive person may begin by doing considerable entertaining and having group studies of his own to air his point of view and win people over to his position. These things can happen in the best of churches, for Satan is ever seeking to disturb their peace and order. Are we watching out for these wiles of the devil, these tricks, by which he will take good people and draw them off the track?

In striving for a sanctified fellowship, what is our attitude and policy towards 'outside' influences? Churches are sometimes very casual about this. Satan desires to sift our whole church, if he can, as wheat. Some pastors are careless in letting their members or their young people's groups be affiliated to the so-called para-church movements. While they struggle to establish a standard of doctrine in the church, they hand their people over to the instruction of these ecumenical, often charismatic organisations. Similarly, some pastors are too relaxed about visiting speakers who are invited to the church, even handing over the task of engaging visiting preachers to a relatively inexperienced person.

What is our attitude to those who come into our fellowship from other churches – students perhaps, if we are in a student area? Some may bring with them serious errors. We will naturally want to minister to them and influence them. Though they may hold wrong views, we will be careful not to shoot them down in flames as soon as they arrive, but we will need to be giving corrective teaching and counselling, or they will never be helped, and they may soon begin to corrupt the biblical views of the young or otherwise vulnerable members.

Do we watch and warn our members about decadent 'evangelical' books and magazines? Sometimes one will go into a sound, reformed church and be quite amazed at the dangerous material offered on the church booktable. The booktable secretary may not even be a church officer, let alone a reader of these books. This is a frightening conduit for corruption and doctrinal subversion in a church. Pastors and elders – do you guard those booktables? Do you warn people to be aware of the campaign being conducted through some of these books and magazines? Or are the people left in naivety and unawareness of these things? And what about some of the 'broadcasts' people follow on the internet, including popular evangelical women preachers who claim to be 'reformed' but include everything from nonsense to heresy in their teaching?

We deal with Christian service next in this book, but it is worth noting here that when a church has keen workers for the Lord, whose priorities are for the kingdom, then a standard of selfless living is exhibited which is the very best example to new believers. Let us pray that the Lord will give us *examples* to the flock – dedicated, loving, gracious elders and senior members – because then a church is three-quarters of the way to being a *sanctified* church, and the young are shaped in godliness.

Paul's Ten Point Design for

Church
Health&
Growth

4

A
Working
Church

POLICY 4

A Working Church

I N SPURGEON'S DAY an American Christian newspaper editor once decided to spend a week at the Tabernacle to make a survey of the great man's ministry. But as this editor surveyed the work of the Tabernacle evening after evening, an entirely unexpected scene met him. The basements and rooms of the building were constantly alive with activity. Groups assembled for district visitation; prayer gatherings convened; ragged school classes were under way; Sunday School teachers' briefings took place, and a host of other activities. This editor came to extol the work of a pulpiteer, but discovered also a *working church*.

Sadly, in many fellowships today, most members loyally attend the services and financially maintain the work, but beyond this they are little more than comfortable observers. On the principle that God uses human instruments, nothing much can be accomplished if we do not persuade as many people as possible to be willingly committed to avenues of Christian service. This is the policy of the working church. It is magnificently spelled out in *Ephesians 4.16*, where Paul attributes church growth to 'the whole body fitly joined together' in Christian service. It is 'according to the effectual working in the measure of every part' that the body secures its growth, and edifies itself in love.

Many local church leaders today say they would love to have vibrant Sunday Schools, but they cannot persuade anyone to staff them. Good Christians have lost touch with the old standard of a working church, and no one wants to be committed to demanding tasks. It may sound unspiritual, but the fact is – no Christian service means no growth. Furthermore, the absence of Christian service eventually leads to an introspective, self-preoccupied, spiritually unfulfilled people, dependent for happiness on self-indulgence in the secular aspects of life.

Let us champion once again the biblical doctrine of the working church, taking special note of the great working verbs of the New Testament. Four great terms are used by Paul to advance the imperative duty of Christian service. First there is the *labouring* term, and it is applied not only to preachers but to all believers. Paul uses it often, a prime example being the promise-laden verse of *1 Corinthians 15.58* – 'Therefore, my beloved brethren, be ye stedfast, unmoveable, always abounding in the work of the Lord, forasmuch as ye know that your *labour* is not in vain in the Lord.'

The Greek word for *labour* speaks of hard toil. It is a strong word, signifying that the worker is pressed with pain. Significantly, this is Paul's most-used term, by which the Lord calls us not to mild service, or only to what is enjoyable to us, but to sacrificial effort for his glory.

A second term used by Paul to describe Christian service is a *striving-contending* word, an athletic term, used to convey the idea of determination and intense effort.

A third term is an even stronger word from the field of competition, a Greek fighting term from which the English word 'agonising' comes. This has in mind the supreme effort required to sprint the last yards of the race, or to escape the crushing hold of a contestant wrestler and turn the tables.

A fourth term used by the apostle is the *aspiring-to-honour* term, showing that Christian people should serve with a level of commitment only achievable because the final crowning day is kept in view. Such terms, in many passages, are the authority for the working church concept.

It is a glorious sight to see a church where the people work willingly to press forward the Gospel and to keep the coals of the testimony glowing hot. There is so much to be done, and pastor and elders will need to initiate a programme, enthuse God's people, train the young, and so implement the work. There is the work of the Sunday School, with its weeknight support meetings. Regular visitation needs to be carried out, and hospitality given, to mention just a few labours.

The voluntary principle must, of course, be honoured in our efforts to draw believers into avenues of service, but once a church is moving forward in this respect, the desire to serve will inevitably spread among the godly, and the hearts of the people will find their true fulfilment. Let us build *working* churches, for these are growing churches, and these are the churches peopled by those whose hearts beat in sympathy with the beautiful words of Frances Ridley Havergal:

> Jesus, Master, whose I am,
>   Purchased thine alone to be,
> By thy blood, O spotless Lamb,
>   Shed so willingly for me,
> Let my heart be all thine own,
> Let me live to thee alone.
>
> Other lords have long held sway;
>   Now thy name alone to bear,
> Thy dear voice alone obey,
>   Is my daily, hourly prayer:
> Whom have I in Heaven but thee?
> Nothing else my joy can be.

Jesus, Master, whom I serve,
Though so feebly and so ill,
Strengthen hand and heart and nerve
All thy bidding to fulfil;
Open thou mine eyes to see
All the work thou hast for me.

Jesus, Master, wilt thou use
One who owes thee more than all?
As thou wilt! I would not choose;
Only let me hear thy call.
Jesus, let me always be,
In thy service, glad and free.

Longer comment on the concept of a working church is assembled in a booklet by the author – *Your Reasonable Service in the Lord's Work.*

Paul's Ten Point Design for

Church
Health&
Growth

5

A
Learning
Church

POLICY 5

A Learning Church

A GOSPEL CHURCH is a wonderful organism designed and brought into being by the Lord, and able, under his blessing, to fulfil many goals. It is at one and the same time an army for the conquering of hearts, and a hospital for the care of souls. It is a community for worship, prayer, sanctification, spiritual labour, fellowship and also for pleasure in the things of God. But there is a central purpose and function assigned to local churches which must never be forgotten, because without it nothing else can develop or stand for long.

This brings us to our fifth great policy aim for the successful building of a true church. We must strive to produce a consciously *learning church*. Paul mentions pastors and teachers who are provided for the perfecting of the saints, building them up in the knowledge of the Son of God 'unto a perfect man', and thus growing up into Christ.[1] Paul also insists – 'Let all things be done unto edifying' – which refers to the building up of the understanding.

---

1   See *Ephesians 4.11-16; 1 Corinthians 14.26; 2 Timothy 4.2.*

The preacher, he says, must preach the word with 'all longsuffering *and doctrine*'. In many passages the concept of constant learning is emphasised by Paul.

A Gospel church is, among other things, a college. This is not said to promote false intellectualism, which gives rise to 'theoretical' believers lacking real character, love and service. Nevertheless, a true church is a place where people love to hear the Word unfolded, its wonders researched and displayed, and the words and plan of God expounded.

We call it a 'college' because this suggests a settled scheme of learning pursued to a high standard, and culminating in some form of qualification. In reality, the ideal church will have very little of the atmosphere and feel of a college, and will certainly not have assignments, examinations and diplomas. However, the teaching elder will have a clear ambition to include, over time, all the counsel of God in his teaching plan. And the people of the church will be conscious that they are pursuing a grand course in divine knowledge, and will revel in the topics, subjects and themes being set before them.

What a shame it is that sometimes people have no consciousness whatever that they are engaged on a study course of sublime truths. Sermons are just sermons. Bible Study meetings are just Bible Study meetings. There is no visible rhyme or reason to them. There is no sense of continuity, nor of any total picture being formed. The minister has been preaching from *Ezekiel* for so many months or years, and when he has completed the series, he will just think of something else, but for no apparent reason.

A learning church is very different because it breathes purpose and progress and accomplishment. The minister would probably never dream of publishing a syllabus, and may not plan far enough ahead for that, but the steady processing of recognisable doctrines and themes assures his hearers that he is carrying out his duty to God and his duty to them in a considered, responsible way. He clearly desires to be faithful, thorough, and comprehensive in his teaching. And he obviously respects them as serious students of the Lord and his Word.

Does the preacher keep a checklist of all that he has done? What doctrines has he preached? What Bible books has he presented? What vital practical themes has he taught? What devotional encouragement has he given? Has he defended the faith, and helped his people to see through the errors of the day? Has he taught the great promises of the Bible, so essential to faith in all the trials of life? Does he privately review his teaching from time to time? Does he keep watch on the time spent on any individual Bible book, so that one is not expounded at such inordinate length that the people have no access to many other parts of the divine study course?

The writer well remembers a pastor being very concerned about a neighbouring semi-charismatic church enticing away his weeknight Bible Study congregation by holding a special training school on the same night. A number of people went off to the other church armed with notebooks and pens to study the Bible course on offer. The deprived pastor realised that his people had no awareness that he too was teaching a Bible course. He soon trimmed his sails, restructured his teaching so that it appeared more purposeful, gave his messages meaningful titles, and distributed notebooks. His weeknight studies breathed new life, and the Word-hungry wanderers returned.

The moral is that it must be *apparent* to people that there is valuable material being taught. It must be *seen* that there is a grand scheme of learning being presented for believers. We repeat, this does not mean that a church will actually feel like a school or college – God forbid! There are massive differences. But it must be sensed that there is a methodical, conscientious process operating in the preacher's mind. The formation of a learning church depends on this *apparent, visible* process being in operation.

Several other factors may also be mentioned as necessary elements in the development of a learning church. The material taught must be *manageable*. The preacher must know how to be profound and yet clear at the same time. Always he must cultivate clarity, so that all can enjoy the deep things of God.

In addition, learning must be *worthwhile*, in that whatever is taught should have a valuable application, either to the individual or to the church, so that it challenges, encourages or strengthens the hearers. Theoretical teaching appeals only to a minority of minds. Learning must also be *enjoyable* and *memorable*. The Christian preacher is handling the most remarkable and wonderful material in the world, and he must exploit its intrinsic power to move and impress the hearer. Ultra-plain preachers should work more on the overall shape of their messages, and be a little less predictable.

Former national servicemen will recall the 'bill of fare' or menu posted outside every mess hall, describing the delights to be served within. But how impossible it so often was to recognise any of that promised fare in the serving tins. How do we, as preachers, prepare and serve the spiritual food elements, in all their variety, of the Word of God? Are the people able to taste distinctive views of the Lord, doctrines, insights, promises, biographies, warnings, comforts, apologetic encouragements and examples?

Do they discover the biblical sources of help for all situations? Do they learn the purpose of individual biblical books? Do they know by name the great doctrines and their purposes? Are they proofed against current Satanic viruses? Are the people able, each new year, to pray in song the words of the hymnwriter –

> *Grant us new beams of light to see,*
>   *New steps of thine to trace,*
> *New visions of thy majesty,*
>   *New visits of thy grace.*

> *Help us new peaks of Truth to climb,*
>   *To grasp new realms of lore,*
> *Each depth divine, each height sublime*
>   *More amply to explore.*
>   *Thomas Hornblower Gill*

Are the people conscious that the ministry they hear is no accident; no haphazard, chaotic process, but a most conscientious endeavour to represent all the counsel of God? We must aim to produce a consciously learning church!

Paul's Ten Point Design for Church Health & Growth

6
An Evangelistic Church

POLICY 6

An Evangelistic Church

IN BRITAIN, countless churches have been lost to the Gospel or closed altogether in the last fifty years, and many of the faithful congregations that remain have dwindled to a handful. Some, in panic, have yielded to church-growth gimmickry, charismatic worship and entertainment-evangelism in the hope that these will save the day. Others seem to await with patient pessimism their approaching demise.

But none of this was ever necessary, if only pastors and officers, stirred by zeal and faith, had sought to inculcate in their people a thirst for and commitment to untiring evangelism. Surely this should be one of the greatest aims of the minister – to build a soul-hungry fellowship of people 'holding forth the word of life'. It is a supreme achievement when pastor and people say with Paul – 'For necessity is laid upon me; yea, woe is unto me, if I preach not the gospel!'[1]

Is this not our burden according to the great commission of the

---

1   *1 Corinthians 9.16*

Lord? Is this not the priority set before us in the glorious history of the *Acts of the Apostles*? Then why, O why, do we deny the Lord by allowing soul-winning zeal to run down? Why do we fail to stir up believing hearts to view their churches as God's light in a dying world? It must be our policy not only to promote evangelism, but to train everyone to be wholly identified with this great aim. Within each congregation solidarity in evangelism should be a most precious objective.

There must be regular evangelistic preaching, preferably one service every Lord's Day being dedicated to the persuasive preaching of the Gospel. This is frequently pleaded for by this writer. When Paul wrote the words, just quoted, 'Woe is unto me, if I preach not the gospel,' he was referring to the soul-saving doctrines of the good news. (We can be sure of this because Paul only ever used the term 'gospel' in an evangelistic context.)

There must also be child evangelism, not just a Sunday School that caters mainly for the children of church members, and that has no clear soul-winning emphasis, but a School which is as large as possible, seeking to draw in all the children in the vicinity of the church.

There must be constant encouragement of personal witness (far and away the principal means of bringing lost people to hear the Gospel). There must be visitation, literature distribution, and whatever other means of spreading the Gospel that the Lord enables the fellowship to undertake. Does it happen in our church?

Here are four aspects of evangelistic effort to which a preacher must give attention as he seeks to build up a right ethos in the church.

1. Every congregation needs to develop a pressing sense of responsibility and calling in this matter, feeling the burden of having received an urgent commission from the Lord. *This* must be seen as one of the great reasons for our existence.

As churches we stand or fall to a great extent on whether we please our Redeemer in our attitude to Gospel proclamation. Indeed, we should even have a fear of punishment or loss should we fail the Lord in witness, perhaps by the forfeiture of privileges. The Lord cares whether we obey him, or disobey. If I am a pastor I must ask myself – What am I doing to encourage a high level of responsibility in God's people?

2. Beyond this sense of responsibility, every true church needs a *positive thirst* for instrumentality in evangelism. All the members should closely follow the progress of all departments of the work, praying much for individual lost people. Foundational to a thirst for instrumentality is deep feeling for the lost. Preachers particularly should constantly plead for compassion to be felt for the lost.

3. Churches certainly need an unclouded view of the free offer of the Gospel, or zeal will be vulnerable to confusing views. Is everyone clear that the sovereign God, who initiates the work of salvation in regeneration, still desires that sinners are consciously convinced by the reasoning of the Gospel? The Spirit alone will make them willing to hear and respond, but persuasive preaching is the external agency.

Conversion is not an unconscious experience. Does everyone in our mainline reformed congregations know why so-called hyper-calvinism is inadequate and mistaken? Is the gracious and convicting tender of salvation to individuals loved, understood and defended? Vagueness in these things soon undermines the pleading tones of the Gospel.

4. In addition, an evangelistic church needs a truly hospitable, welcoming spirit, and a readiness to patiently parent babes in Christ.

All these virtues begin with the pastor and officers. A minister or ruling court should never nominate for any kind of office a man who possesses a heart of stone in regard to evangelism – or who has never been conspicuous for soul-winning zeal.

What is our policy for training the fellowship in zeal, support-iveness and undying, unflagging effort to bring people under the sound of the Gospel? The minister who neglects to build a right attitude among the people will soon find himself a lone warrior in evangelism, discouraged, unprayed for, and unsupported by a witnessing flock. But one who leads the way, by evangelistic preaching, by keeping alive the soul-winning flame in all departments of the church, and by manifesting a clear love for and thirst for souls, will surely build a like-minded fellowship. May the desires expressed by Charles Wesley be ours also:

> *Now, Saviour, now thy love impart,*
> *And govern each devoted heart,*
>   *And fit us for thy will;*
> *Deep grounded in the truths of grace,*
> *Build up thy rising church, and place*
>   *This city on a hill.*

> *O Lord, thou dost thyself inspire*
> *Our hearts with this intense desire*
>   *Thy Gospel to proclaim;*
> *Thy glory only we intend,*
> *O let our deeds begin and end*
>   *All done in Jesus' name!*

> *Except thou, Lord, shalt bless the plan,*
> *Our best conducted schemes are vain,*
>   *And never can succeed;*
> *We'll spend our utmost strength for nought,*
> *But if in thee our works are wrought,*
>   *They shall be blessed indeed.*

> *Now make our faith and love abound!*
> *O let our lives to all around*
>   *With drawing lustre shine;*
> *That they our blessedness may see,*
> *And come to seek their all in thee,*
>   *Thou saving Light divine.*

Paul's Ten Point Design for

Church Health & Growth

7

A Separated Church

POLICY 7

A Separated Church

IN EVERY AGE some churches of Christ have been lured into association with those who taught or practised some fatal corruption, leading to their ultimate falling away from evangelical purity. The story of the last century has been a history of tragic loss for Bible-believing congregations in Britain. First to fall were thousands of churches in the historic Protestant denominations, so that the latter now have only a handful of truly evangelical churches remaining in them. Bible-believing churches, reluctant to secede from these denominations when they capitulated to theological unbelief, were themselves taken over by it.

Association with error proved to be the death of them. Their young aspiring ministers went off to liberal denominational colleges to be ruined, churches became small and closed, and their assets and properties passed into the hands of their theological enemies. Today, the devil campaigns to destroy all remaining evangelicalism but with a different strategy. Instead of infiltrating the denominations with the unbelief of liberalism, he insinuates a heavily-modified evangelicalism of his own invention. This is the so-called *new evangelicalism*, with its weak view of salvation (which includes acceptance of Catholic 'salvation'); its compromised view of the inspiration and authority of Scripture; its denial of creation, and even (frequently) of eternal punishment; its worldly lifestyle, and numerous other wrongs. It is more dangerous than blatant liberalism, because it claims to be Bible-loving and supportive of the new birth, but while it uses the language of Zion it has departed from Bible Christianity in many ways.

This viewpoint, hand in hand with new-style worldly worship and charismatic folly, now devours conservative evangelicals everywhere. It has never been more important for churches to recognise errors which undermine the faith, and stand clear of them. Those who dabble with Lausanne-style new evangelicalism invariably succumb to it. Those who are indifferent to danger will be taken over.

Since the time that Balaam counselled the Moabites to intermarry with the seemingly invincible Israelites in order to bring them down, infiltration and compromise has been Satan's chief strategy for the destruction of faithful evangelicalism. Yet so many believers recoil from obeying the biblical commands to stand clear from error. Pastors and leaders who seek acceptance within spiritually decadent circles will be responsible for the ultimate ruin of their churches. There must be separation from worldliness, and from all forms of seriously wrong doctrine.

In the 1960s and into the 1970s a clear note was being sounded in Britain about the error of belonging to denominations dominated by unconverted, Bible-deriding, anti-evangelical teachers. Today, however, that clear note has almost disappeared. Nevertheless, *2 Corinthians 6.14-18* is still in the Bible, and it remains the command of God. Paul's words must be our policy:–

'Be ye not unequally yoked together with unbelievers: for what fellowship hath righteousness with unrighteousness? and what communion hath light with darkness? and what concord hath Christ with Belial? or what part hath he that believeth with an infidel? and what agreement hath the temple of God with idols? for ye are the temple of the living God; as God hath said, I will dwell in them, and walk in them; and I will be their God, and they shall be my people. Wherefore come out from among them, and be ye separate, saith the Lord, and touch not the unclean thing; and I will receive you, and will be a Father unto you, and ye shall be my sons and daughters, saith the Lord Almighty.'

If people teach, for instance, that Roman Catholic allegiance is equivalent to evangelical conversion, so that the pure Gospel is no longer the exclusive means of salvation, they deny the faith, and we are commanded by God to separate from them and to warn against their teaching. (This means we should also turn away from their books.) If we do not, then all the plausible excuses imaginable in the world will not alter the fact that we will have spurned point-blank the command of God. We will have become (as Scripture says) partakers of the offender's sin, and if we are pastors or elders or deacons, we will doubtless have jeopardised the spiritual safety and health of God's people.

This does not mean that we cannot fellowship with other believers because we differ on such matters as baptism and church government. We will rightly keep to such distinctives in our own congregations, but these differences do not tear down the faith. The new evangelicalism, however, marks an erosion of vital matters, and the essentials of the faith are rocked to their foundations. Nor does separation mean we cannot have fellowship at a personal level with Christians who are caught up in denominational or new evangelical churches. Our quarrel is with those who wilfully promote the wrong, and associate with it, not with unenlightened rank and file followers. We long to win them from those circles, and they are not the guilty teachers. Biblical separation is always a careful and sensitive act.

It must be our aim to teach our churches the necessity of biblical separation from all wrong teaching which undermines crucial doctrines, and to ensure that every member knows the bedrock texts which establish this prime duty and act of loyalty to God. These are shocking days – times of spiritual high treason even among some professing servants of Christ. But where is love for the Lord, if his people are not protected in the way he has prescribed? Where is love for Christ, if his churches are handed over to his enemies? Where is love for the Word, if the ministries of its critics and detractors are admired and embraced? 'Shouldest thou help the ungodly, and love them that hate the Lord?' *(2 Chronicles 19.2.)*

Our aim must be to strengthen and protect the people of God from capture by plunderers, and this is secured by self-conscious and enlightened separation from false teachers and their pernicious ideas. To fail in the teaching of separation is to commit the ultimate cruelty of preparing the Lord's sheep for the slaughter. We are described in Scripture as 'saints', meaning *sanctified,* or *set apart* for God. And we cannot be set apart *for* God without at the same time being set apart *from* sin, worldliness, and the enemies of Truth.

Some ministers in the past have practised biblical separation as far as their personal associations are concerned, and they have guarded their pulpits, but they have not given their churches any insight into their policy. The people have received no warning ministry, and have therefore developed no clear convictions on this matter. Tragically, when their faithful pastor has left the scene, they have yielded, in naive trust, to their spiritual foes.

Voices are raised today uttering the now hackneyed adage that we ought to be building bridges rather than erecting walls between Christians, but this is lamentably foolish counsel when it is advanced in preference to the plain commands of God's holy and infallible Word.

In the 1870s the 'Downgrade Controversy' engulfed the Baptist Union of Great Britain. Professors in the Union's theological colleges, as well as prominent ministers, denied essential doctrines, and escaped removal or censure. C. H. Spurgeon protested, urging discipline, but he went unheeded. Conscience-bound to obey Scripture, he separated from the Union over its refusal to repudiate denial of essential truths, and called faithful ministers to do likewise. Over the years, many did so, but the vast majority chose to make no stand for Truth, and to remain. The result was the decimation of that once great company of fervent churches by the forces of liberalism. Scarcely anywhere today is there to be found a 'union' church which is firmly for the Gospel and the Word. Failure to stand for the Truth led to dreadful consequences. There are times when separation alone represents love for Christ, love for the Word, and love for the cause. There are times when separation alone will preserve the buildings which former generations of godly labourers have left behind.

The wise and discriminate application of biblical separation calls for a longer treatment than is provided here, and the writer trusts that readers will not mind his suggesting to them his booklet – *Stand for the Truth.*

It is an essential part of our policy – as it was of the apostle Paul – to introduce the careful, thoughtful, prayerful and faithful implementation of biblical separation, including separation from wilful new evangelicalism. Without this, there can be no long-term spiritual quality in a church, and no stability. Biblical separation is certainly not *negative*, as some suggest. It is as positive as any cleansing, preserving process, for it keeps alive precious purity and biblical obedience in the churches of Jesus Christ. We should never lose sight of the fact that we are 'saints', or those dedicated and committed to the Lord and to his Word.

Paul's Ten Point Design for

Church Health & Growth

8

A Sacrificial Church

POLICY 8

A Sacrificial Church

ONE OF THE most beautiful and vibrant characteristics which can be produced in a congregation is a sacrificial spirit, and we should greatly desire and work for this. A sacrificial people fulfil the principle of *Romans 12.1* – 'I beseech you therefore, brethren, by the mercies of God, that ye present your bodies a living sacrifice, holy, acceptable unto God, which is your reasonable service.' Whether we think of monetary giving, or the stewarding of time and energy, all is readily yielded to the Lord's work by those who have a real sense of how much they owe, and this sense is stirred by Christ-exalting ministry.

The great enemy of the sacrificial spirit today is the comfortable lifestyle which has become a basic human right. An almost unconscious covetousness and acquisitiveness can creep in among even the best believers, making them soft and self-pampering to some degree. Gone are the days when the poorest believers would painfully yet gladly tithe, filling envelopes with cash, and marking them for various missionaries. Yet it should be possible for a ministry to gently bring a congregation back to such a full-hearted surrender to the love of Christ. Unless, sadly, a minister inherits a congregation which has gone too far down the broad road of self-seeking and self-consideration, it should be possible by God's blessing to rekindle the spirit of sacrifice. Here are a few factors to be borne in mind.

1. Total commitment must be the preacher's theme

The *substance* of our offerings of service and stewardship are precious to the Lord, but most precious of all is the willing, sacrificial spirit behind them. 'Willing' is the key word in this objective, and so the preaching ministry must be conducted with great sensitivity, not commanding and demanding, but moving and persuading the Lord's people over time to yield themselves wholly to him.

2. Early teaching is best

The ideal time to be educating believers to the duty of stewardship is at the very beginning of their Christian lives. Among other materials, this writer gives to young Christians, and to applicants for church membership, a copy of the booklet: *Christian Stewardship – Our Calling.*

3. Service leads to stewardship

If we can move believers to make a willing sacrifice of time and energy in *practical service* for the Lord, then the stewardship of substance will follow almost inevitably. Some churches – especially if they do not have a vigorous evangelistic Sunday School – give little opportunity to members to serve the Lord, which is a serious disservice to him, and also to those members. It is inevitably a blow to sincere stewardship because this grows best out of practical service, and a spirit of sacrifice.

4. Show the great change in affluence

We have already mentioned the affluence and comforts of life today, and this should lead us to have a special understanding and concern for younger Christians. The era of affluence arrived quite suddenly, and those who have come to adult life *since* its arrival have no 'feel' for the newness and unreality of it all. The luxuries of yesteryear are the necessities and basic rights of today. In the booklet just referred to I wrote the following paragraph:

> 'Today we have so much. Our youngest earners drive cars of a newness and quality that their peers of only thirty years ago could not even dream about. Our newly-weds generally start with all the appliances, and more, that their parents had to acquire gradually on the long march to middle age. The humblest home seems to have hi-fi and video equipment, plus money for substantial holidays, and so on. Yet, from what we hear, churches and pastors around the country frequently struggle financially, and disturbingly few significant ventures in local evangelism can be put into motion.'

We must put the new era into perspective for younger believers, so that they may see the full scope Christians have for reasonable simplicity of life, and for giving.

5. The influence of example

Example is extremely powerful either to fan the spirit of sacrifice to a bright flame, or to extinguish it. People cannot see what we *give*, but they can certainly see what we *keep*. And they can surely also see what we *do* for the Lord. If the leaders of a local congregation drive luxury cars, those who are commanded by God to accept their rule and example will follow similar worldly aspirations.

The writer knew a church situated in a run-down urban area, which had a small forecourt on which were parked at service times the ultra-smart, upmarket vehicles of the elders. These were far more prominent than the notice board, with its Scripture text. What did this say to the members – particularly new believers? Did it fracture their God-given, instinctual feeling that a believer should be reasonable in lifestyle in order to be a great giver? Of course it did.

If middle-aged members of a congregation (to pick an unlikely example) speak about their expensive cruises, will their juniors rest content with more modest holiday arrangements? To preachers also we must breathe a brotherly warning – What you *say* will be far less influential than what you *do*, when it comes to stirring up a sacrificial spirit. 'Be thou an example of the believers,' commands the apostle. What if some members do set a bad example – what should be done? First, of course, friendly persuasion is the way, and certainly not carping, sniping, allusive remarks made in the public ministry.

Reasonableness in lifestyle opens the way to sacrifice. And once spiritual generosity is embraced, it, in turn, sustains reasonableness, because a sacrificial spirit is the very best curb to covetousness, and a great spur to contentment.

6. A noble objective is needed

Sacrifice needs the encouragement of significant spiritual objectives. Our first objective is, clearly, to please and honour the Lord who bought us. But sacrificial Christians also need to know that their giving will accomplish great things for the Lord. It is hard to sacrifice for nothing. So, what is our church doing? Is it preaching only to the members? Are there insufficient Gospel objectives at home and overseas to secure the wholehearted longing of the members?

Carey's famous dictum, launching the nineteenth-century missionary movement, was 'Pray – plan – pay', and pay they did, from full hearts. The very first 'collection' for Carey's fledgling mission was from a group of ministers, and the people soon followed. Prayer for blessing accompanied by planning and sharing of aspirations quickly inspired sacrificial stewardship. True believers are willingly inspired by worthy visible efforts to bring glory to their Lord and King.

7. The gifts must be seen to count

Sacrifice also needs the assurance that gifts given at great cost are not squandered. If a church is one of those that never does anything itself, but *every* time brings in the builders, decorators, and even the cleaners, the spirit of sacrifice can hardly be fostered. But where a more frugal spirit prevails, and God's people do what they can themselves so that resources may be applied more directly to the King's business, then the sacrificial spirit is encouraged.

Significantly, it is true of sacrificial stewardship (as it is with avenues of practical service) that 'where your treasure is, there will your heart be also' *(Matthew 6.21)*. Our stewardship binds us in love to the cause, stimulating prayer and concern for the promotion of the work, and motivating us to settle any problems that arise in a responsible spirit, so as to preserve that which is so precious to us. In other words, a sacrificial church is a peaceful church.

Paul's Ten Point Design for

Church
Health &
Growth

9

A
Loving
Church

POLICY 9

A Loving Church

I T IS RATHER EMBARRASSING to be extolling the glories of a *loving, caring* church as the *ninth point* of this study, because such an objective surely deserves a much higher place on our policy agenda. But nearly all the ideals for church life may be said to deserve a higher place.

For a fellowship to possess mutual, affectionate and caring love is to honour the 'new' commandment of the Lord. The apostle John declares that it is an 'old' commandment, and yet (for the fledgling Christian church) new in its practical achievability and bonding power *(1 John 2.7-8)*. Paul, in *Ephesians 4*, calls for lowliness and meekness, with longsuffering and mutual forbearance in love. This, he says, is the only way to 'walk worthy of the vocation wherewith ye are called'. How much we should desire for our church an atmosphere of mutual kindness and concern! How glorious it is to know that this can be accomplished! How important it is to preserve and nourish it, once produced!

It is far more likely that a *serving church* (by contrast with an uninvolved membership) will become a loving church, because fellowship in service produces deep ties, and because the possession of a common, higher objective subdues the possibility of petty hostilities. The quest for brotherly love does not require a programme of fellowship events, church rambles, suppers, and so on. Churches that fight and squabble often have all these activities in abundance. Fellowship in service is the best bonding agent for believers.

Love for our fellow-believers is one of the proofs of conversion, and it is certainly essential for pleasing the Lord. Six times in the Greek New Testament love is described by the word *philadelphia*, meaning – brotherly love. Internal clashes and divisions must go, and *philadelphia* love must be cultivated. Respect for one another is not enough. Nor are consideration and kindness, important though they are. The Lord commands the depth and tenacity of love equal to that seen in a blood tie. We must have 'brotherly love', a key 'policy' in all the epistles *(Romans 12.10; 1 Thessalonians 4.9; Hebrews 13.1; 1 Peter 1.22 and 2 Peter 1.7)*.

A vital reason for the cultivation of mutual love in a congregation is seen in the Saviour's great prayer of *John 17.21* – 'That they all may be one; as thou, Father, art in me, and I in thee, that they also may be one in us: that the world may believe that thou hast sent me.' As a local church we are intended to reflect the character of God, including the sublime love which exists between Father, Son and Holy Spirit. Our 'family' likeness must be derived from above, and this will bring down witnessing power. Surely this must be an overriding concern of pastors.

Another reason for cultivating congregational love as a priority is that the local church is the dwelling-place of God, through the Spirit *(1 Corinthians 3.16)*, and cannot be blessed if it is not a fit place for God to dwell. The presence of affectionate, caring love is the essential 'environment' for the habitation of the Spirit.

We remember, also, that the Lord is training every local church to be a family, not merely a group of individuals, and the greatest quality of a family is love. Dare we frustrate the purpose of Christ by indifference to this grace?

We remember further that love is a 'parent grace' in the sanctification process. Without love for other members of our spiritual family, sanctification will falter, and we shall become increasingly self-interested, self-concerned, self-serving and often self-pitying. We may also become jealous of others, critical and hostile. But true sanctification builds love early, taking our minds off ourselves, and bringing us to mind the things of others.

Yet another reason for making love a priority is that without real affection between its members a church can never produce the working efficiency of *Ephesians 4.16* – 'From whom the whole body fitly joined together and compacted by that which every joint supplieth, according to the effectual working in the measure of every part, maketh increase of the body unto the edifying of itself in love.' Indeed, the *level* of effective service carried out by a congregation depends upon the depth of this mutual affection (and at times forbearance) arising from *philadelphia* love. Such love cannot easily be disrupted or shattered by jealousy, gossip and the other hostilities so often fanned into flames by Satan.

Successful cultivation of a beautiful plant usually depends on the soil, and this is true of the development of brotherly love. In this case the essential soil is a *regenerate* church. It is so sad when a fervent ministry and a group of true believers tries to flourish in the midst of spiritually cold, self-righteous, nominal or indifferent people, because these have been admitted as members of the church without giving evidence of true conversion, and without having received the new nature. In such a case, *real* spiritual love can only exist among the truly converted portion of the members, thus producing an ungainly thing – a church within a church. The full expression of congregational love is inhibited.

We need, as teachers, to explain this love, and to apply the pastoral exhortations of the New Testament to hearts in encouraging and practical ways. We need, as leaders, to set an example of hospitality to all – not just to those like ourselves. We may need to quietly propose and prompt acts of hospitality among members, and to find kindly ways of dissolving cliques. We may also need to initiate visitation of the sick and needy by other members, teaching God's people to watch out for each other.

A practical summary for promoting brotherly love

Congregational brotherly love will be advanced by the following acts, aims and attitudes, pursued in prayerful dependence upon the help of the Lord:

1. We must be utterly convinced that the promotion of brotherly love is an essential act of obedience to the command of the Lord.

2. We must view ourselves as children of God who have been placed by the Lord in a *family*, the local church, and charged to contribute to its peace, and promote its interests.

3. We must strive to make the local church a holy, beautiful and harmonious fellowship, fit to be the dwelling-place of Christ, by his Spirit.

4. We must believe that Christ requires us to worship, learn and serve him in a *corporate* way, as one body in Christ, and not to function in an independent manner, which is the sin of pride.

5. We must submit to the obligation to have the same forgiving attitude to our spiritual brothers and sisters that Christ has so graciously shown to us.

6. It must be our sincere aim to suppress self-love in all its evil aspects in order to cultivate unselfish, outgoing interest, affection and support for our fellow-believers.

7. We must make every effort to express affection and regard to others, both in warm greetings and friendliness, and in deeds of helpfulness and kindness.

8. We must also engage in regular intercession for our fellow-believers – for their spiritual and physical blessing – and do so in an

intelligent way, taking account of their ever-changing situations.

9. We must ensure that we remain approachable by others, always at their disposal as members of the same family.

10. We must suppress gossip and evil-speaking, and keep unviolated that priceless bond which God has set between us, always keeping up respect, and protecting one another's reputation.

11. We must be sensitive to the great responsibility which is upon us to keep ourselves pure in the matter of *example*, so that we shall not be judged for infecting the church with unbrotherly, unfaithful and corrupt relational attitudes.

12. We must drive away from our minds jealousy, envy, bitterness, evil suspicions, and all other attitudes which cause us to disparage fellow-believers without proper cause.

13. We must be impartial in all our relationships, and always try to 'cast the net' of hospitality and friendship to an ever-widening circle of people, and to different kinds of people, and not restrict our friendship to a few.

14. We must never abuse the local church fellowship by taking mean advantage of its affection, kindness and resources, and offering no sacrifice of service or care in our turn.

15. We must support as a matter of duty Christian service activities organised by our church, which both bring glory to God, and also promote fellowship, for these people are our people, and their God is our God, and to serve and fellowship with them is a leading duty and delight.

[The above summary is contained in the author's booklet, *The Goal of Brotherly Love.*]

A hymn from a young Baptist pastor in eighteenth-century London summarises *philadelphia* love perfectly:

> *How sweet, how heavenly is the sight*
> *When those who love their Lord,*
> *In one another's peace delight,*
> *And so fulfil his Word!*

When each can feel the other's sigh,
    And also bear a part;
When sorrow flows from eye to eye,
    And joy from heart to heart;

When, free from envy, scorn, and pride,
    Our wishes all above,
Each can the other's failings hide,
    And show a kindred love;

When love in one delightful stream
    Through every member flows,
And fellowship and kind esteem
    In every action shows.

Love is the bond divine that binds
    The happy souls above:
May we, as heirs of Heaven, find
    Our hearts so filled with love.
                                Joseph Swain

Paul's Ten Point Design for

**Church
Health** &
Growth

10

A
Believing
Church

POLICY 10

A Believing Church

FAITH TOWERS over all other Christian duties throughout the Bible, and the preacher or leader who omits the conscious and careful nurture of congregational faith misses a paramount pastoral objective. Our longing should be that our congregation as a whole will have unwavering confidence in the faithfulness, provisions and promises of God, and trustingly obey him in all things.

Congregational faith is encouraged and extolled frequently by Paul in his epistles. Individual faith is the life-blood of the believer, but congregational faith is also a high and precious grace in the teaching of Paul. When he lists the corporate virtues of the Corinthian congregation, he writes – 'Ye abound in every thing, in faith, and utterance, and knowledge, and in all diligence, and in your love to us.'[1] He looks forward also to their corporate faith being increased.[2]

---

1   *2 Corinthians 8.7*
2   *2 Corinthians 10.15*

Writing to the Philippians, Paul describes their faith in action, despite persecution, as a sacrificial offering.[1] He has in mind the faith of the whole congregation, and he rejoices immensely to think of it. Concerning the Thessalonians, Paul remembers without ceasing their (corporate) work of faith, and labour of love.[2] He speaks of how Timothy brought his news of their (corporate) faith and love.[3] He thanks God that their collective faith 'groweth exceedingly' and that all the churches have praised God for their faith (as a congregation) under persecution and tribulation.[4] He is surely still speaking about them as a whole congregation when he prays that God would fulfil in them 'the work of faith with power'.[5] Congregational, collective or corporate faith is a glorious apostolic aim and policy.

Solid confidence in the Lord and his Word is a vital precondition for blessing upon churches, just as upon individuals, as we are repeatedly told in Scripture. Who are the people who may rejoice in the knowledge that the Lord will defend and vindicate them? It is exclusively those who put their trust in him *(Psalm 5.11)*. Yet the frightening reality of our time is that the trust of God's people has been undermined and sometimes even destroyed by faithless workers who have substituted human inventions for the ways of God's Word.

The promoters of modern methods effectively tell us that we do not have to trust the power of the Word and the Spirit of God any more, because their clever systems and super-gifted people will give the desired results. In their eyes their ingenuity has eclipsed and supplanted the backward, stumbling, slow, inadequate habits of former times.

We are now called to trust entertainment techniques with the

---

1 *Philippians 2.17*
2 *1 Thessalonians 1.3*
3 *1 Thessalonians 3.6*
4 *2 Thessalonians 1.3-4*
5 *2 Thessalonians 1.11*

aim of closing the gap between the church and the world in order to attract a reluctant generation. We are urged to trust dance and drama (and the 'Jesus' film). To stir stony hearts we are told to trust spectacular gifts such as healings and prophecies. Famous evangelists have long insisted that we should trust ecumenical cooperation to get the crowds. Leading pastors press us to trust in a new, liberal, worldly lifestyle for Christians as the means of holding the young.

The reality is that faith, on the part of congregations, is a dying grace. Many pastors report that they cannot persuade even genuine Christians to attend times of prayer, because they seem to have lost their once-strong conviction that these are worthwhile, and that prayer will be powerfully answered. Pastors also report great difficulty in raising teams for visiting the community and rounding up neighbourhood children for Sunday School. Why should God's people have become so reluctant to do these things? It is surely because people have lost their trust in the usefulness of such labours, and are no longer excited by the certain prospect of a blessing from God upon them.

Yet, what can be more pleasing to God than faith – not in money, nor our abilities, nor great pastors, nor groups of churches – but in him? We are saved by faith, and we are subsequently blessed throughout the Christian life by faith. We are called to walk by faith. The worldly modern methods we have mentioned have no doubt been permitted by God as a test of our faith – a test so often failed. How may we go about the work of promoting faith?

1. A conscious aim

We should pray and long for the unity of the congregation in deep trust in biblical methods, and in the power of God to magnify and use them. To encourage this, faith and faithfulness must be prominent themes in our sermons. Both Old and New Testaments provide examples of God blessing faithful people. Equally, the Bible is full of promises, and these must always have prominence, not just in their individual relevance, but also in their congregational and Gospel outreach applications. Certainly we must also emphasise the integrity, love and power of the Saviour to keep his promises. Every so often we should reflect, 'In what way am I currently fostering congregational faith?'

2. No ministry of despair

In these dark days there is a tendency for some pastors to paint such a picture of godless society that the people of God think all is utterly hopeless unless a great revival should come, or until the Lord returns. Stark realism this may be, but the picture is not matched by the exposition of the power and grace of God to save, and by his promises to work mightily in the most adverse situations. We must avoid falling into a ministry of total despair which crushes congregational faith. In our darkest moments, our motto-text should be – 'But where sin abounded, grace did much more abound.'

3. Prayer meetings

We have already considered the place of prayer, but it is important to see that faith is not only a prerequisite for prayer, but a fruit of it also. Persistent prayer must be the greatest feature of our church life, second to hearing God's Word. Encourage individuals to attend, and teach this as the key to blessing. Soon the hand of the Lord will be seen, and faith will grow even more. Be careful to bring every great trial or hindrance to the work of the church straight into the prayer meeting, for such things are appointed by the Lord that we may prove him and obtain a blessing.

4. Careful cautions

Warn, but never in a caustic, superior or combative style, about the modern gimmicks and trends mentioned earlier in this chapter. Do not do this so often that people no longer listen, or take such warnings seriously. But as teachers clearly motivated by a desire for souls, and the preservation of God's ways, carefully explain where all these antics go wrong, and why this is so important. These things undermine faith in the Lord, and our people must have light on them.

5. Keep a balance

Even in the life of a faithful church some practices and activities may slide across the line between trust in God, and trust in means. Games and refreshments and outings used in young people's activities can easily become excessive, as though success depends upon the scale of these things.

The use of visual aids in teaching, and the reasonable occasional use of videos and other helps may easily become excessive. We mean well, but are we crossing the line? Is impressive technology laying bare in us a rundown of faith in the spoken appeal under the blessing of God? We must keep all supplementary helps within bounds, and be sticklers for 'proclamation', dependent on the power of God. Let us jealously guard our faith at all costs. A gentle leadership hand on the tiller is often needed, but the ideal is to impart understanding at the same time.

* * *

By the blessing of the Lord the goal of congregational faith will be achieved. It will become increasingly evident that the beauty of solid trust in the Lord characterises our church. We will become a 'believing' church, fixed and rooted in an enlightened way in God's methods.

Every so often we meet a person known to us in previous years as one who stood firmly by conservative principles and ways. However, times change, and this person now smiles in a rather superior way and tells us that he is 'more broad-minded' than he used to be. It becomes apparent that he has moved on from trust in biblical methods, and has gone along with the 'progressive' ideas of worldly Christians. Another person who has gone the same way looks sadly at us and claims that he became 'battle-weary', and so learned to put 'Christian love' and 'liberty' before minor scruples.

Many Christians are sliding into modern alternatives to trusting in the power of God. If we are leaders, we must be urgently committed to safeguarding our people for the Lord. May he help us to bring about through our ministry and unwavering example *believing* churches, pledged, solid and loyal to the Truth and the ways of the Lord, and living under the promise – 'The Lord, he it is that doth go before thee; he will be with thee, he will not fail thee, neither forsake thee: fear not, neither be dismayed' *(Deuteronomy 31.8)*.

The pre-eminence of faith in the life of the church is clearly seen in *1 Timothy 1.5* – a perfect affirmation for conclusion: 'Now the end of the commandment is charity out of a pure heart, and of a good conscience, and of faith unfeigned.'

Imitating the Apostle

'Thou hast fully known my ... purpose,' wrote Paul to Timothy *(2 Timothy 3.10)*, meaning his policy or design or blueprint for the establishing and building of churches. The ten policy points outlined in these short chapters can be clearly established as Paul's own from many references in his letters. Some of these have been cited, but there are many others not referred to here, and together these show that these ten principles were major features and priorities in the apostle's personal methodology.

With these great aims we are safe because they are God-given and part of the pattern of apostolic conduct which we are commanded to follow. Says Paul – 'Brethren, be followers *[literally: imitators]* together of me, and mark them which walk so as ye have us for an ensample *[literally: pattern]*.' He also writes, 'Those things, which ye have both learned, and received, and heard, and seen in me, do: and the God of peace shall be with you.'[1]

The Lord will certainly be with us. To follow the schemes, policies and gimmicks drawn up by mere men – however well-intended they may be – will lead to ultimate disappointment and disaster, but to draw our objectives and methods from the infallible Word will bring us surely under the promises of God, and the power of the Spirit will rest upon us, bringing true conversions, genuine hearts, and all the fruits of righteousness.

---

1   *Philippians 3.17* and *4.9*. See also *1 Corinthians 4.16* and *11.1*.

Booklets referred to in this book
(*Sword & Trowel* publications)

Christian Stewardship

This booklet studies Christian stewardship under a series of helpful headings. So much spiritual blessing is lost when stewardship fails. The author seeks to draw Christians into the full blessing of giving themselves wholly to the Lord.

The Goal of Brotherly Love

The great goal is 'Philadelphia' love – a tenacity of love equal to the love of a blood tie. What obstructs this among believers? What steps must be taken to promote and preserve it?

Stand for the Truth

This gives the biblical arguments for separation from false teaching, showing the positive value of this. Ten commonly-heard arguments in defence of 'inclusivism' (co-operation with Bible-denying groups in, for example, evangelism) are answered.

The Power of Prayer Meetings

Shows why corporate prayer is commanded by Christ and given unique promises. Includes practical advice on the form of the meeting, and the style and content of prayer. An appendix shows why women should participate.

Your Reasonable Service in the Lord's Work

Designed to inspire church members to seek avenues of service within the church, this focuses on the strong exhortations to Christian service in the New Testament. A call to embrace the concept of a working church. For all readers.

Church Membership in the Bible
61 pages, paperback, ISBN 978 1 870855 64 8

Christ has designed a 'home' or family for his people, described in these pages as an accomplishment of divine genius. This is a magnificent subject, vital to spiritual growth and blessing and also to our service for the Saviour. This book answers many questions about churches and church membership in New Testament times. Next to having a real walk with Christ and knowing the doctrines of the faith, membership of a good church has a powerful formative influence on the believer's life.

Worship in the Melting Pot
148 pages, paperback, ISBN 978 1 870855 33 4

'Worship is truly in the melting pot,' says the author. 'A new style of praise has swept into evangelical life shaking to the foundations traditional concepts and attitudes.' How should we react? Is it all just a matter of taste and age? Will churches be helped, or changed beyond recognition?

This book presents four essential principles which Jesus Christ laid down for worship, and by which every new idea must be judged.

Here also is a fascinating view of how they worshipped in Bible times, including their rules for the use of instruments, and the question is answered – What does the Bible teach about the content and order of a service of worship today?

Physicians of Souls
The Gospel Ministry
285 pages, paperback, ISBN 978 1 870855 34 1

'Compelling, convicting, persuasive preaching, revealing God's mercy and redemption to dying souls, is seldom heard today. The noblest art ever granted to our fallen human race has almost disappeared.'

Even where the free offer of the Gospel is treasured in principle, regular evangelistic preaching has become a rarity, contends the author. These pages tackle the inhibitions, theological and practical, and provide powerful encouragement for physicians of souls to preach the Gospel. A vital anatomy or order of conversion is supplied with advice for counselling seekers.

The author shows how passages for evangelistic persuasion may be selected and prepared. He also challenges modern church growth techniques, showing the superiority of direct proclamation. These and other key topics make up a complete guide to soulwinning.

For a full listing of Wakeman titles please see www.wakemantrust.org